Copyright © 2018 Tekkan
Artwork Copyright © 2018

All rights reserved.
First Printing, 2018
ISBN 978-1-7324107-3-2

To contact Tekkan please email:
buddhaboy1289@gmail.com

Table of Contents

Utopia. . . . . Page 97

How to Read My Poems

I have married the sonnet to the tanka. I tell a story in the sonnet — using three quatrains, separated by line spaces, and a final couplet. The story builds to a conclusion in the couplet. The tanka is a commentary, or a counterpoint, to the sonnet — the combined poems have two endings.

I don't rhyme my sonnets, because I want freer expression. I want to be direct in my meaning — I want people to clearly understand my meaning. The metaphors are inspired by Shakespeare, and the (aimed-for) precision is in imitation of Japanese style. Using the sonnet with the tanka, I am mixing the sensibility of the Occident and the Orient — which I have done by living in England, Japan, and America.

I don't punctuate much in my poetry. I want the words themselves to do the work. There is logic between words, and the forms provide structure. By not using punctuation I hope to direct readers to carefully attend to each word — to appreciate the graininess of words.

Reading my poems silently, say, on a bus, a train, or an airplane, and reading them aloud, may be different experiences. The way I've written there's not always a pause intended at the end of the line. Hint: *My poems are to be recited not as lines, but as phrases, and a phrase often overflows the break at the end of a line. I pause and take a breath where it seems natural for me to pause. Another person may pause differently than I do.*

Each single poem is a piece of a mosaic, and it is my hope that the collection of poems form an accurate portrait of consciousness.

My daughter, Jocelyn MacDonald, is a wonderful artist. Her art work graces this book.

I am Barry MacDonald. I received the *dharma* name, *Tekkan*, which means, Iron Man, a settled practitioner of great determination.

— *Tekkan*

Everyday Mind IV

Watching sails on
Lake Biwa from
Mount Hiei — thoughts go
all the way home to
Stillwater Minnesota.

There are words said over centuries at
Zen temples and they are intended to
Puzzle and ensnare thinking but like a
Jackrabbit solutions are evasive —

A monk waited in line for an hour
And he entered a room with a bell and
Waited until the master finished with
Another monk and the master rang his

Bell so the monk rang the bell before him
And on his way down a long hall he passed
The previous monk and on arriving
He bowed three times and he kneeled before the

Master who asked him "What is the color
— the original — color of your heart?"

Speech is limited
during practice periods
at Zen temples and
silence creates solitude
engendering clarity.

Driving down a hill in Stillwater to
Meet a friend at a coffee shop in a
Hurry because a late frosting in spring
Made me take the time to scrape my windshield

And wanting to be on time and having
Only seconds to spare I noticed that
The rising sun looked like a silver disk
Within a fog that filled the broad valley

And it seemed a cloud had descended to
Occupy all of downtown while the air
At my home on the north hill was crystal
And even though I was rushing I fell

In love with my hometown and it didn't
Matter my friend forgot the appointment.

I lived in Oxford
England and in Kyoto
Japan and other
places but I discovered
where my roots have taken hold.

There are times when I'm habitual and
Not attending carefully but doing
What I do everyday at the same hour
And I need an explosion to awake

But when I'm conversing with a friend I
Get to hear his experience and see
With his vision and in the process of
Sharing I discover the turnings I've

Taken and the growing I've done that by
Myself I could never have recognized
Because the conversation reveals what's
Meaningful and it seems we have a much

Broader perspective together than we
Do separately and life becomes fun.

I am a talking
animal created for
conversation and
if I'm not conversing I'll
probably fall off a bluff.

There are the people who have the power
Who know the law and the traditions who
Operate behind closed doors and there are
Corporations with lobbyists and there

Are bureaucracies making rules and law
Enforcement agencies acquiring
Information and there are journalists
Who write for journalists who despise the

People they should be informing and the
Nation is divided between a small
Number of politicos who have the
Influence and the majority who

Struggle to understand what's true in a
Profusion of deceitful narratives.

Everyday a new
storyline is broadcast to
the nation about
whom we should all hate and
what is the correct thinking.

It was just a twig hanging in the air
Yesterday but a bud is appearing
Today as it's swaying in a bitter
Wind and it's necessary even in

April to bundle up because spring has
A hard time coming in Minnesota
And I can see the tips of the maple
The walnut and cottonwood are budding

Even though the overcast sky is dark
The branches look barren the air is cold
Moist and heavy and a persisting wind
Is lacerating my skin but I see

The grass is stubbornly rooted and thick
On the ground and assertively greening.

Today the birds aren't
singing or perching in trees
they're darting about
because what else can they do
in a bitter April wind?

April is in a single drop on the
Sill of my window and April is in
The nascent buds of the trees that appear
Mostly barren and in the chilly air

And in the overcast sky and in the
Misty horizon — and April is in
The reemerging dampness and in the
Water pooling in my basement again

And every year I know what to expect —
It's time to put away the snow blower
To sharpen the blades and change the oil of
The lawnmower — and I'll look for the day

When the sun nourishes everything but
Today is a mess of saturation.

The crooked little
apple tree is growing a
profusion of limbs
reaching up in the air and
it's my job to remove them.

I won't say it's age as I remember
It happening in my thirties and I
Rely on my memory but sometimes
I would enter a room and realize

I'd forgotten why I came — and I think
It's the result of an active mind that's
Processing too much information and
There's calculation going on and as

My mind is juggling several things at once
Such as the immigration policy
Of the United States and my desire
For toothpaste — naturally my mind would

Drop the ball concerning the paste and that's
OK because my capacity for

It was inspiring
scintillating even and
I was on the verge
of a pronouncement but then
the brilliant point escaped me.

The sun is shining through the tiny leaves
Of the cottonwood making them yellow
With light revealing them for the first time
All the way up the height of the tree and

The leaves are brilliant in the blue of a
Sky without clouds and the intensity
Of the sun that's already well up is
Hard to face without shielding myself with

My hand and I notice a halo of
White surrounding my fingers and I see
All the emerging leaves of the trees are
Shining yellow and I'm puzzled how it

Could be that the air is as chilly as
November as the spring is arriving.

I have to slow down
to cultivate enough of
the necessary
patience before I can see
the flow enveloping life.

I've always looked up to people not in
Admiration but because I'm five-foot
Two-inches tall (not) and to overcome
My stature I became an exercise

Nut running up and down a twelve story
Building thirty times and for the last five
Times I ran up every other step — but
Such deeds didn't make me taller — but now

I'm a youthful almost sixty-year-old
Not sorry I overcompensated
For so long but I've learned everyone has
Something about themselves they regret and

As good as it is to earn self-respect
It's better to become compassionate.

With the advancement
of technology we may
all reach the age of
one-hundred-fifty years —
may we all become raisins!

I would not have gotten where I am now
Without discipline — though I'm not sure that
I'm entirely happy with where I
Am now — because it's not easy to get

Up at 5 a.m. and do the lotus
Posture for forty minutes or in the
Afternoon do cardio exercise
For an hour everyday day and once I

Acquired the discipline its easy
To become much too rigid about my
Routine as if the practice were the point
But the point is liberation and the

Practice is a method and direction —
How would it feel to be liberated?

The ancestors wrote
everyday mind is the way
and liberation
and practice are one so I'm
trying to understand them.

I measure progress by upping the weight
Of the barbells I lift and I do a
Frantic tempo on aerobic machines
Outdoing the young guys and I enjoy

Looking svelte and muscled because without
Exercising at sixty years old I
Could be dilapidated overripe
And depressive and I keep coming to

The gym because I want a sharp mind and
An elevated spirit because I've
Taken far too long to awaken to
The magic and mystery of life and

I want to apply the discipline I've
Won to explore with curiosity.

I could be cranky
and cantankerous
but my body is
a maserati
rumbling and ready.

I've been an exercise nut from the age
Of thirteen with a facility for
Building muscle by lifting weights — but I
Also like to eat so I get chubby

In the middle which I don't like so —
Three times I went on a diet and lost
Fifty pounds eating less and slimming down
Each time assuming a mission watching

Every morsel checking with a mirror
And nothing was more important for a
Year but then my appetite betrayed me —
So I went from lean to pudgy again

But last time I learned about nutrition
And now I'm slimmish by eating smartly.

No matter how much
austerity I impose
I can't keep going
forever so it's better
to think as much as doing.

Usually my name is Barry but
For a joke I'm calling myself Bernard
Because I want to watch my friends say hey
Who is that guy because I want them to

Come to me and ask who are you — and I
Will say I don't know — who do you think I
Am — so together we can find who I
Am because sometimes I don't know and

I want my identity to be clear
Not just an assortment of attributes
And attitudes of relationships and
Memories because it's easy to say

I am something but it's like casting a
Spell and I believe I am what I say.

Do I claim my name
or maybe my history
perhaps my desires —
I do have a direction
but don't know where I'm going.

I live for the optimism that comes
With the morning as the light permeates
My surroundings and I can see how the
Leaves are unfolding today transforming

A barren landscape to fruition and
Just for a moment the quarter-grown leaves
Of the cottonwood are thrilling in a
Brisk wind and the light has turned green into

Yellow and the open sky imparts a
Sense of endless possibility and
I want to be here and I don't have to
Do anything extraordinary for

The moment but watch as a couple of
Birds chase each other and then disappear.

It's not a feeling
that I could do anything
that inspires me
but that I recognize I
don't need much to be happy.

I was groggy when the alarm went off
And Johnnie the cat was letting me know
With is his most insistent yowling coming
From under the door he wanted his food

So I fed him and the other cats changed
Water in three dishes vacuumed around
A litter box cleaned two litter boxes
And then I washed dishes and made coffee

And I made the bed and got dressed I read
My meditation books and finally
I ate my breakfast cereal and was
On the verge of showering when I saw

It was midnight I only slept for two
Hours and the alarm didn't even ring.

Johnnie the feline
interrupted my dreaming
and I'm ready to
go at 12:00 a.m. but
everyone else is sleeping.

Even if I'm driving down the same streets
Every day there's a chance I'll discover
Something I've never seen before if I
Pay attention to the flowing world as

I believe there's always more than I can
Absorb in the moment as my habits
And preoccupations get in the way
And today I saw the willow trees at

The chilly beginning of spring and the
Profusion of drooping limbs are hanging
Limply looking like yellow strings with leaves
Emerging and my imagination

Jumps with the sight of willow leaves flowing
In the resurgence of summer breezes.

I've seen the willows
for almost sixty years —
nothing resembles
the flowing world better than
willow leaves in summer wind.

With each breath comes a tang of water
In my nostrils and everywhere the rain
Is drumming and it isn't drizzling
This is a warm shower and the trees are

Enshrouded in the downpour and the leaves
Are budding again the grass is greening
Again and earthworms are emerging in
The puddles of my driveway again and

This is the day of the threshold of growth
As the earth is absorbing the moisture
And even though the sky seems heavy I
Am happy because it was a grueling

Winter because I was indoors too much
And now the sun will trigger everything

The sky is clearing
a breeze is rising and a
finch is bobbing on
a cottonwood twig and
all the birds are flying.

I assumed the dirt was always filled with
Earthworms and I see them when turning soil
For the garden or during a downpour
When they turn up on the sidewalk or the

Driveway and then they dry and get crispy
Which puzzled me so I spoke to my friend
The ecologist who said they can't breathe
When the ground becomes saturated with

Rain and they're not native but were brought by
Fishermen as bait and they spread eating
Nutrients and depriving the forests
Of sustenance and eventually

They will return the land to grasses and
Put a stop to their voracious feeding.

The worms are out of
control and taking over
like the mafia
infiltrating a village
of innocent citizens.

That the worms will eat until the roots of
Trees disappear and grasslands emerge that
Little worms will determine what the birds
And animals do that earthworms with their

Tiny mouths will mindlessly consume so
Much over passing decades that the earth
Will regenerate — as worm sustenance
Diminishes and their numbers return

To equilibrium — makes me wonder
Apart from what people do what else is
Happening — from what other direction
Will metamorphosis come making the

Future unpredictable because so
Much is going on all at the same time.

I see the world
only as it is
but don't have
a clue where it
is going.

The phones with little speakers that I plug
In my ears — allowing me to listen
To music during the ordeal — and the
TVs positioned about the room — and

The second-story windows — are meant as
Distractions from the monotony and
The revulsion of my exercise at
The gym — and I'm tired as I mount my

Partner the elliptical machine as
I always measure ability and
Effort against time and supposed distance —
And I know exactly what I'm in for —

I will push as much as possible and
Hopefully I'll come again tomorrow.

The yoga pants the
women are wearing while
exercising are
stimulating but they don't
overcome my suffering.

The small room is used for storage now though
The cutting and folding machines are there
With the Ryobi printing press and the
Containers of chemicals and the cans

Of ink enough to print but the press has
Been idle so if I put the rollers
On the pressures between them would be off
And even if adjustments were made and

I inked up the quality compared with
Laser copiers would be hard to match
As the machinery is obsolete
And I miss the rhythm of the running

Press and remember years of effort and
Acquired skills and earned satisfaction.

My dad decided
to print his publication
himself but he's gone
and I am the publisher
and turned to Bayport Printing.

Even the boundaries of my lawn are
Rectangular and every room of my
House is a box and my roof is made of
Triangles and everything about home

Is far from avant-garde but it's plopped on
A globe revolving on its axis and
Rotating around a sun that's just a
Little star among billions of stars and

I don't know what it's all about but I
Feel right at home in my neighborhood in
My city of Stillwater because it's
A quiet and friendly place to watch as

People come and go and the seasons bring
Changes and I'm trying to stay awake.

If I take the time
to absorb the expressions
and words of people
there's a lot to consider
as everyone's a puzzle.

I could make a list of things that went wrong
I could get up in the morning to gripe
About someone and I could nourish a
Grudge from yesterday or ten years ago

But there's no end of that sort of thinking
Once a victim mentality takes root —
But this morning I'm on a mission to
Leverage the clarity that comes after

Meditation to seek inspiration
To cultivate intuition — and with
A settled mind I see the sparkle of
The sunlight among the new grown leaves of
The cottonwood as they're turning in a

Breeze and feel joy in the observation —
Without the peace I wouldn't see visions.

The trick is leaving
my concerns behind for a
moment forgetting
my identity to let
the flowing world enter me.

I am a driving animal who sees
Nature going by who stopped on a road
While mommy and daddy geese with goslings
Decided to cross which made me ponder

Dignity as I recalled the day I
Gazed at a goose and it looked at me and
I wondered what could it think with such a
Pinched little head and then it hissed which was

Discourteous and as the family
Ambled sedately on attending to
Their business unconcerned with impatient
People I granted them admiration —

Without a smidgen of embarrassment
The caravan waddled majestically.

Sometimes a goose is
unflappable and
sometimes a goose is
irascible — who
am I to quibble?

I have my group of sober drunks who I
Meet down the hill from my home five minutes
Away and they give me their laughter and
Ears and over the years in the same room

I've met a parade of broken people
Who just want the hurting to stop — and some
Grow and others go — and it's amusing
How in the beginning we are islands

Of buried treasure and with the practice
Of communication isolation
Vanishes and potentialities
Blossom with expression as I witness

Anger confusion and shame melt away
And confidence and direction emerge.

There's no predicting
how productive energy
will bloom as she may
celebrate motherhood or
become an entrepreneur.

We were given a couch — the kind that's a
Fold-away bed — and wanted it in the
Basement but on the way we came to the
Corners to the stairs and standing it on

End we angled tilted shoved swore and yanked
But the steel frame wasn't flexible and
Lifting was exhausting and balancing
On the stairs was precarious and I

Tore a favorite shirt on a nail I had
Never noticed before and though we were
Hot and frustrated we weren't finished and
I can't say how and doubt whether we could

Do it again but there it is in the
Basement — a reminder of victory.

When the time comes for
the couch to go it won't go
as a couch but in
pieces because I won't go
through the ordeal again.

Each day comes with opportunity and
Firstly I have to feed and brush the cats
As I'm conversing with them because I
Am a talking animal and then I

Attend to water dishes and litter
Boxes and take out the garbage and make
Coffee and while I'm moving my thoughts are
Popping as my mind is waking up and

I enjoy the liveliness of thinking
And I may be looking for solutions
To problems or pondering the meaning
Of someone's words but I'm discovering

What's important for me today and I
Can determine how to use energy.

My thinking creates
direction and impetus
when leaving my home —
I want to be curious
I'd like to be flexible.

There's no substitute for the belonging
And the joy I get from sitting with my
Circle of sober drunks as we exchange
The tricks involved in shifting the habits

Of mind away from taking a drink or
Drug because after one there's no control
Of how much of what happens and of whom
We hurt and we may never get sober

Again — addiction is inescapable
Unless our mentality is transformed
And it takes a drunk to help a drunk and
Together we're strong in isolation

We perish so we focus our lives and
On practicing spiritual jujitsu.

An invisible
and untouchable power
gives me impetus
and addiction vanishes
and we rejoice together.

Arriving at the gym as I do in
The afternoon everyday I opened
My bag to discover two jerseys and
No short pants — so I returned home in a

Fume — and I removed my shoes at the door
So as not to trail in the mud behind
Me and I grabbed my shorts and returned to
The gym but then I realized the shorts

Were nowhere inside the car so I drove
Home again in befuddlement and found
The pants on the kitchen table and it
Seems in the act of retying my shoes

Where I was and what I was doing was
Not important enough to remember.

Sometimes there's a hole
Where common sense should
be so I will try
to remember to do
one thing at one time.

Having a memory is like walking
With a loaded library in my head
And it's possible to know why I so
Often say or do what I do based on

My experience but I don't want the
Compulsion of doing the same things in
Similar circumstances and I think
It's much easier to remember my

Disappointments and injuries and then
My thoughts are punishing — but I want to
Recall the faces and voices of my
Friends and relive those moments when we were

Floating along like clouds and life was fun —
And then my head becomes a treasury.

There is so much
accumulated
experience that is
useful if I have
poise.

Mac Barlass was a wonderful man — he
Was kind cheerful and unselfish and
He was persistently optimistic
And he always came prepared with a joke —

I am in Pioneer Park on a bluff
Overlooking Stillwater watching the
St. Croix River thinking about all the
Tributes at Mac's funeral and thinking

About his reliable smile and his
Words of encouragement seeing the sun
Playing on the surface in ripples of
Light and seeing other places where the

Water is glassy seeing the river
Flowing down the valley to the ocean.

It's easy for me
to be inspired with the
sun and the sky but
night is intimidating —
vastness without oxygen.

Nature is intriguing offering new
Visions everyday as the trees flower
As birds appear and there are coyotes
And foxes about but it takes careful

Attention to see them and people fit
Within the realm of nature too but we
Are subtle and confusing because we
Behave according to unique patterns

Of mentality we establish for
Ourselves and some of us have whirlwinds in
Our heads and others are serene but each
Is busy with thoughts and emotions and

Communication does take attentive
Practice and not everyone's capable.

I aspire to
the poise
of a samurai
awake and
ready.

If he weren't shut in he wouldn't have the
Urge if he weren't bursting with energy
And if the outside weren't so enticing
With so many smells and sounds and if there

Wasn't the magic of an unexplored
World expanding in all directions with
Strange things moving about he wouldn't be
Poised at the door tensed and ready to spring

The moment there's an opening and though
He doesn't like the snow the rain isn't
An impediment so we have to be
Awake when entering or leaving the

House because if we aren't quick enough the
Blur of an escaping cat will be out.

He likes to go to
the basement window and roll
in the dirt and he's
not bothered at all by
the presence of the bees.

In Japan I know it's golden week when
Cherry trees and wisteria bloom and
The air is clear and I remember the
Streamers of carp flowing in the wind as

Japanese celebrate the respite in
May between the penetrating winter
And the oppressive humidity and
They gather in the parks and spread blankets

Under the blossoms of cherries that bloom
Briefly and disperse and memories of
My moments under those trees arise when
I'm driving in Stillwater seeing the

Apple crabapple and cherry trees as
The blossoms are passing by in a week.

Americans don't
appreciate flowering
trees as the bloom of
days vanishes before we
notice but I celebrate.

Of all things they are marks of a moment
Passing in a week in cheery shades of
White pink and red lighting the landscape with
Subtlety that only attentive eyes

May appreciate that make me think of
Candy canes and ice cream and taffy that
Prompts a quiet celebration and that
Returns me to my years in Japan where

They celebrate appropriately the
Blooming trees — and then I see the apple
Crabapple and cherry petals flowing
In the wind and Stillwater returns to

The ordinary hues of the leaves and
The grass and the clouds the sky and the sun.

The dandelions
with yellow blooms
with balls of white puffs
and with deep roots
aren't as likeable.

Sunday

After a glorious afternoon with
An open sky with the warmth finally
Descending everything was bathed in a
Glowing and in the clear air everything

Was visible and the earth was fresh and
Now that the sun is gone the air is just
As clear and the moon shine is brilliant and
Even though they are enveloped in night

The white and pink and red blossoms of the
Flowering trees are prominent for a
Person who enjoys passing visions of
Ordinary miracles and even

Though there's work to do tomorrow I'm here —
Caught again in springy resurrection.

Each leaf is pristine
because the bugs haven't yet
begun nibbling —
everything is visible
because it's not yet humid.

What sort of warrior places kindness
Above assertion generosity
Over belligerence and what are the
Benefits resulting from attending

To the daily passions of life with the
Intention of being harmless doing
Good? I have practiced long enough to know
When I'm angry or frustrated when I

Want something just because I want it or
When I get upset because I'm telling
Myself a story that's probably false
And I understand I have to be poised

Because thoughts and emotions are wayward
Because I'm seeking clarity and peace.

Because I am a
spiritual warrior in
a flowing world and
I'm balancing my troubles
and trying to stay awake.

Every sort of warrior prepares for
Battle and a testing of skills and strength
Against opposition for the purpose
Of conquest but the word "enemy" is

Paradoxical because whom does a
Spiritual warrior confront except
Himself and what is the struggle apart
From the disturbance arising within

His consciousness and if clarity and
Peace are the point a peculiar kind of
Skill and strength is necessary — watching
The arousal of anger and letting

Go without harming anyone because
Anger is only a passing phantom.

Being disturbed and
behaving with excitement
are easy to do
and the universe responds
to erratic emotions.

Anything can happen in the flowing
Universe from a driving accident
From the malicious intention of a
Stranger or from a cough developing

In cancer and the unpredictable
Could happen to me or to one I care
About and there's no defense and it does
No good to be morbid so I practice

Gratitude in simple pleasures minding
My breath coming and going watching a
Woodpecker on the cottonwood seeing
That the leaves are tiny but taking shape —

I see the earth is bursting with life and
I appreciate it's living magic.

I don't have to
wonder how I would feel if
I weren't so afraid
because I'm not afraid and
I believe life preservers.

There's a fire in the sky today and the
Newly grown leaves are attuned to the fire
And the grass is rising up and as I'm
Turning in a circle there's the sparkle

Of the sun everywhere among the leaves
Turning in a breeze and the blue of the
Sky without a cloud appears as a dome
Lit by a disk so bright I can only

See it in glimpses and I imagine
Myself as a leaf buoyant in the wind
Absorbing warm energy but as I
Don't have ability to turn off my

Thinking I can only aspire to
Momentary poise — then go back to work.

There are mornings when
the sun is drenching the earth
making everything
appear fresh as if time stopped
and beauty is eternal.

Once I'm going one motion flows into
Another and I'm able to yank the
Cord as many times as necessary
To start the mower for the first time in

May and I pace behind the motorized
Wheels that set the pace and on the hill I
Have to tilt while walking and I mow as
Much as possible around the rocks that

Border several gardens and this year I'll
Have to trim the lower branches of the
Trees because they've become impediments
And with every step I'm treading over

Familiar ground and I can day dream or
Cogitate but I enjoy the motion.

When trimming the grass
around the rocks bordering
the gardens with the
weedwacker I pretend I'm
a tyrant mowing rebels.

I don't consider there's more computing
Power in the phone I carry in a
Pocket than in the Apollo rockets
That took astronauts to the moon — when I

Routinely talk to people across the
Country while walking along the street or
Get directions by using satellites
Or download wisdom accumulated

Through centuries by connecting with the
Internet — all by using a phone — I
Don't give technology a second thought
And even become frustrated with a

Slow connection as I've grown accustomed
To the magic people have provided.

And it's easy to
forget separate from
the wind in the leaves
and beyond the sky
another star's exploding.

It's not easy to focus my thoughts on
The questions I would ask if I met you
But the chance of our meeting again is
Unlikely because I'm not seeking you —

I want to know why you eagerly shared
So much and what it was about my words
That touched you and kept you responding for
Years as we explored in conversation

But the disregard of breaking off as
You did revealed however much I
Gave it wasn't enough for you and from
The beginning I was wanting more than

You could give so what's there to say beyond
Saying hello I hope you are happy?

I've discovered my
capacity for giving
unselfishly but
I need better discernment
and a little more patience.

I meet my friends in the morning and for
A laugh I'll pretend to be limping with
My left leg and then I'll limp with my right
Just to see if they're paying attention

Or I'll stand behind one of them and lean
One way and then the other and I don't
Need to use words to enjoy myself — I
Don't even know I'm smiling — but when I

Have to take a photo of me and I'm
Manipulating my cell phone trying
To capture the perfect spontaneous
Smile I'm more likely to smirk or even

Grimace because suddenly it's very
Difficult to put on a happy face.

I stretch my lips and
narrow my eyes and
raise my cheeks and
make the final effort and
lift the corners of my mouth.

The grass greened and buds emerged on the trees
During the chilly and rainy days of
April and this year I noticed all the
Limp willows in Stillwater turned yellow

And then there were the mornings without clouds
When the sky and the sun became magic
When nourishment descended from the sky
And the earth was baking in clean warm air

And the cherry apple and crabapple
Trees bloomed again and the grass grew again
And now lilacs tulips and irises
Are blossoming and the leaves are fully

Grown and I'm waiting for a blustery
Day to hear the wind stirring leaves again.

If I'm not awake
I won't even notice the
everyday magic
constantly emerging
consistently evolving.

Eating Out

I enjoyed my strawberry salad with
Grilled chicken and walnuts and French dressing
Because I exercised and was hungry
While you were animated and needed

To tell me about Barbara about
How she told everyone she was giving
You her hours because you were so poor and
Needed help and Barbara was rude and

Barbara de-friended you on Facebook
Again and you're really going to look for
Another job and I don't remember
What else you said but you noticed me as

I was already finished eating and
You were irritated and feeling rushed.

I tried to appear
attentive as I knew you
didn't want advice
and I tried to stay awake
but I wasn't successful.

When I look broadly at the world I see
Wicked people appear to prosper and
Hurricanes blow indiscriminately
And it's easy to believe there is no

Basis for optimism and yet I
Have created a foundation for my
Life by waking early and feeding the
Cats and then I meditate drawing strength

From within and without and then I go
About my business with clarity and
Inspiration comes — like snatching a bird
In flight with my eyes — and I know there is

A freedom of choice with consequences
And then a possibility for growth.

I touch and
Manipulate
Everything
With my mind
And everything responds.

I sit quietly letting thoughts come and
Letting them go and as I'm practicing
I understand there's no control of a
Thought arising but I don't have to take

Ownership and the trick is learning to
Release disturbance and to awaken
Poise and patience and I've become aware
That the earth communicates with me and

When I see the new-grown leaves tossing in
The wind and I hear the sighing of the
Wind passing through the leaves I realize
The ever-present trees from my childhood

Have always been whispering messages
Of consolation and of contentment.

My mind tells me to
manipulate people and
make things happen but
the trees are whispering don't
worry everything's OK.

Meditating Together

The rain sounded on the tin roof of the
Cottage and we were sitting quietly —
Each of us absorbed in our separate
Realities in the warmth of the room —

And I listened to the pattering of
Rain and to the undulations of a
Woman and a flute harmonizing and
I could not distinguish any words but

The music summoned in me a hunger
For a love I couldn't identify
A love not tied to appearances and
Not dependant on circumstances but

A love establishing a lifetime of
Peace — I hungered for original love.

I was yearning for
a womanly form
of softness and warmth —
no distinguishable words

While walking near the Apple River in
A steady rain I saw a fishing boat
Filled with dirt and implements once drawn by
Horses — a boxy combine and a plow

With rotting wooden handles — and I thought
About the stamina it took to turn
Soil with a small blade and I saw
The rooted wilderness in riotous

Growth and my feet were soaked from treading the
Sodden ground and I realized that the
Countryside doesn't ask anything of
Passersby but the farmer here had to

Apply the uttermost of himself and
Today his tools are rusting in the grass.

A single raindrop
would leave ripples in water
for a moment but
in a downpour the drops
are vanishing without trace.

Rain drumming on a tin roof provides a
Soothing rhythm for our day together
As we've rented the cottage for this day
As we've planned our gathering beforehand

But we couldn't control the weather and
Even though the pattering above makes
Us speak up and lean in to be heard I
Love the sound of rain on a roof because

It allows me to feel sheltered — and we
Ventured out with umbrellas to take part
In a soaking afternoon to enjoy
The revival of spring together and

Here I am with sodden socks and bare feet
Thoroughly contented among my friends.

Swallows flitting and
geese and goslings paddling
about the river
aren't discomforted by rain —
but they don't have my cold feet.

Routine sustains me as I follow my
Feet entering my car and returning
To where I was yesterday and taking
My place in the circle of sober drunks —

There's a way out of alcoholism
But not every drunk can follow the way
Because it demands turning inside out
Attitudes emotions and impulses —

I'm one of the lucky drunks because I
Prefer talking honestly about what's
Going on today to having secrets
Because communication is healthy

And isolation leads to resentment —
I'm not that much different from anyone.

Usually I'm
listening to another
drunk propounding a
nonsensical story that
I perfectly understand.

It's Memorial Day honoring the
Sacrifice of generations and I'm
Reminded warfare is continuing
While in Stillwater we relax on a

Radiant day while I'm watching the clouds
Drift while I see a formation of geese
And hear them honking and I wonder where
They are going and why together and

How do they choose a leader and does he
Decide direction and when they pass I see
How rapidly the clouds are moving and
Everywhere the earth is resplendent with

Spring while there's much I don't understand as
Today is the epitome of peace.

If I had suffered
trauma and
carried memories
could I be here
peacefully?

A white disk with a tinge of yellow is
Ascending in an empty sky and my
Skin is absorbing the heat and my head
Is feeling dazed with the force of the sun

And the trees that I watched in winter that
Stood in beseeching postures with barren
Branches uplifted in frigid air to
An overcast sky that were images

Of hardship and supplication are now
In foliage and every leaf is tasting
The sunlight and the sky is blue and the
Leaves are green and the splendor of summer

Has come round again bringing fruition
And who could stand by without rejoicing?

The frosting is gone
the earth is digesting rain
the sun is stirring
growth and the roots are drinking
minerals and nutrients.

Seeds of the cottonwood are opening
Floating and disclosing the quality
Of air as puffs are descending slowly
And outwardly from the tree and a puff

Is caught in a breeze and goes for a ride
On the impetus of a summer wind
And I wonder whether it's the light or
The temperature that triggers the tree

Maybe the culmination of moisture
In the soil plays a part in prompting the
Releasing of the seeds as I'm aware
Of the layering on of the years as

I watch a drifting and flowing puff as
It discloses the quality of time.

Everyday
everywhere
everything
is flowing
in a breeze.

In the Florida everglades pythons
And alligators lurk in the grass and
In the north bears amble in the forest
And they gallop and they scamper up trees

But if I were escaping I'd run down
A slope because their front legs are stubby
And they'd stumble downhill and if only
The earth were a mountain I'd be OK

But I deplore the wood ticks that sneak in
The grass drop on skin and burrow in with
Sharp little legs and pincers to suck blood
And transmit lime disease so the earth does

Not resemble paradise and even
The minutest parasite is nasty.

They are stems and leaves
with thorns for most of the year —
only in spring with
a showering of the sun
are roses ethereal.

A slight stirring of wind is enough for
Leafy shimmering and I can see June
In the yellow reflection on each of
The cottonwood leaves and I can see the

White disk with yellow radiance as the
Sun is setting as heat is lingering
In the air and to the east the sky is
Pale and the leaves of trees are a dark mass —

I am a remembering creature with
Images of the snow in the wind in
My head with knowledge of the summer and
Winter solstice incessantly coming —

I'm knowledgeable enough to use words
And to appreciate a summer sun.

The sun swelters in
July and early August
and the grass burns and
turns brown and humidity
makes my breathing difficult.

Craig

You are a remembering animal
Telling me about the moon and you and
The black wolf considering each other
Telling me about the fifty deer you

Shot as the climb is demanding as we're
Treading a plowed field traversing woods
The forgotten barbwire and the brambles
Telling me about the albino fawn

You saw and as we reach the pinnacle
Of the ridge with a view of forty miles
You see a kneeling deer three hundred yards
Away that was invisible to me

Because I have eyes used to streets homes and
Parks and you gave yourself to the country.

You talk about the
verge of grass between the plowed
fields that keeps the soil
from eroding downhill as
the deer enters the woods.

When I was thirteen my dad led me out
Of the house by the front door and said if
You don't work for me you'll ruin your life
And I thought there's no way that's happening

And I was angry at the presumption
Of the right to determine my life and
I resented the intrusion he made
In my mind though at the time I couldn't

Put my thoughts into words and I didn't
Know the tradition of the eldest son
Taking over the family business that
Propelled him as I was caught in a net

That however much I resisted he
Established the arena of conflict.

Only because he
was a publisher and I
was able with words
did I consent to become
his printer and editor.

I decided not to be my dad and
Would not repeat the drama he imposed
And I didn't want to determine the
Personalities of my kids but watched

Over them as parent's do so when a
Dentist told me Joshua as was eating
Sugary gummy bears I was shocked so
I started saying "Joshua brush your

Teeth" and through elementary junior
High and high school I said "Joshua brush
Your teeth" and he appeared compliant but
He wasn't brushing and a crescendo

Of cavities resulted while he was
In college and I was given the bill.

My dad was a
bunker buster bomb
penetrating deep
reaching the foundation
blasting permanently.

The responsibility of forming
A persona is inescapable
As we aren't solitary animals
And we depend on each other for the

Roles we play the status we bestow the
Love we give and receive and everyone
Hungers for esteem and affection and
Everyone measures themselves by sizing

Up other people and appearance and
Ability and elasticity
Determine how I show up in a group
And what I think about myself and it's

A puzzle each of us has — what are the
Tricks that will get me what I think I need?

Putting the best foot
forward comes naturally
from the earliest
years and I don't think about
forming personality.

My body and abilities are gifts
And I've made use of curiosity
And honed a facility with words to
Probe experience with intuition

But sometimes I feel separated and
Misunderstood and I create stories
And hypnotize myself with self-pity
As I portray myself as a victim

And sometimes I see sunlight reflected
In cottonwood leaves and listen to a
Friend talk about loving a woman and
Hear how a sober drunk encourages

Himself and I remember I'm happy
When I stop demanding just what I want.

I am flesh and blood
and my thinking produces
visceral moods
so I have to be patient
and attentive and gentle.

The power went out in the night and the
Alarm didn't ring but my body has
A timer telling me to get going
So I went through the morning routine in

The dark feeding and watering the cats
Cleaning the cat box in the basement by
Using the dawning light through a window
And shaving in the dark and checking my

Success with my fingers tips and I thought
About the refrigerator and I
Considered how soon the food would spoil and
I was grateful my cell phone was charged but

Without electricity I couldn't
Have what I need — I couldn't make coffee.

Did the demented
North Koreans explode a
missile covering
the entire Midwest with an
electromagnetic pulse?

Our destination is Baraboo in
Wisconsin and they in Chicago and
We in Stillwater Minnesota leave
Early in the morning to meet half way

Between at the Log Cabin restaurant
As we've done for years and we talk on the
Highway as rolling hills farms and big rigs
Go by and we talk when we arrive for

Lunch in small town America because
We share a cultural political
Point of view and we bring to the table
Our differing experience and our

Various livelihoods and together
The conversation is exploration.

Conversing about
political issues is
an American
tradition worth pursuing —
we believe in liberty.

The everyday lying that goes on in
Politics that serves to define villains
To be hated and the righteous who are
Lionized is nauseating to watch

Because I know that the narratives are
Aimed at hypnotizing the masses who
Don't understand the intricacies of
Policy who vote because they're afraid

And angry and the perpetrators in
In the bureaucracies in Congress and
In the press work together to present
Their self-serving version of the truth with

Supercilious airs and whoever
Opposes them is accused of hate speech.

Occasionally
one of the ruling class will
tumble from grace and
with spontaneous words they
expose self-pity and rage.

Reading the newspaper seems old fashioned
Since the Internet speeds the news in the
Air instantly to a laptop or a
Phone feeding an appetite for breaking

News or the latest snarky opinion
And there are so many commentators
With so many competing interests
It's hard to separate the truth from lies

And there are so many people taking
Advantage of the trillions of dollars
Floating around the economy and
Working for it seems old fashioned when it's

Easier to leverage power and trade
Influence within established circles.

News is purposeful
to foster paranoia
to infuriate
to incite tribal instincts
and to protect the powerful.

The morning is for meditation and
Poetry and I leverage clarity
To explore the flowing world arising
And dissipating in sunlight in wind

In trees in budding and undulating
Leaves where I don't have to make judgments and
By the mid-morning I'm striving to make
A living by publishing a journal

Of political opinion my dad
Started fifty years ago and by noon
I'm consumed with personality in
The realm of fighting devils where people

Lose balance while seeking dominance and
Power and all I see is bitterness.

This morning of the
summer solstice the sun is
illuminating
a flowing mountain range of
clouds and nothing else matters.

There are months when thinking about money
Isn't consuming because I send the
Fundraising letters and the money comes
In and the cash flow is seasonal so

I know when the account will be drained and
The publication dad founded fifty
Years ago has weathered the ups and downs
By building a base of subscribers who

Are loyal because they appreciate
The classical liberalism we
Promote that advances liberty that
Opposes the bureaucratic state but

During the days when money dissipates
It feels like a python is squeezing me.

I leverage
morning clarity
for inspiration
playing with words and
hunting the possible.

In Middle America with about
A thousand subscribers I edit a
Journal of ideals and my writers live
Across the nation and I have little

Influence on politics and know a few
Politicians but I understand how
Systems function how wealth is created
And squandered and I've become familiar

Enough with history to believe no
Matter how much prosperity we have
Civilization is precarious
Because the people who exercise the

Power of government usually
Are people who enjoy using power.

Dissimulation
intimidation
manipulation
are useful arts of
successful power.

The most important job I have is in
Keeping my spirit up as I could be
Making a better living doing a
Dozen other things than publishing a

Journal of opinion especially
When the ideals are misunderstood but
The effort resembles a mission and
I believe it's good work — but when money

Is at lowest ebb pressure builds and I
Recognize I'm in the same boat as the
Countless owners of small businesses in
America and if they can summon the

Necessary courage to persevere
Than I can find the guts to continue.

I meditate in
the morning to leverage the
clarity to put
my words together and to
keep my spirit soaring.

For the publication to succeed I
Want to offer a view of events that's
Inspiring and my writers provide me
With history showing magnanimous

Personalities and they school me with
Economics demonstrating how the
Discipline of choice ennobles people
And it's child's play for me to assemble

An issue addressing today's problems
With yesterday's or last millennium's
Solutions and we don't have to engage
In vitriol and accusation so

Typical of the twitterverse because
Our readers crave healthy encouragement.

The opposition
manipulates the envy
and ignorance of
people and their solutions
have failed again and again.

We talked before dawn on the phone you
In your bed and I in mine separate
But communing almost every morning
For more than two years and I waited for

Five a.m. lying awake for when I could
Hear your voice again telling me about
Every little thing and I was inflamed
And excited as never before at

The age of fifty-nine as I explored
What passion was as I discovered how
To express thoughts and emotions that I
Didn't know were buried in me and we

Never ran out of things to say until
You got yourself a real relationship.

I was addicted
to a woman I couldn't
possess and I wonder
is the excitement worth
the ragged end of passion?

The fear was in my stomach and back on
Tuesday when I was thinking about the
Future without any surety of
What or who will be with me — and ragged

Fear was the acid hollowness in my
Gut — was the tension in my back — but like
Any emotion does the fear dissolved
And today I'm drawing encouragement

From the gentleness of the breeze in the
Leaves and I'm wondering if love is like
The wind the water and the light as love
Is transparent by itself and only

In relation to something and someone
Else does love emerge to soothe my spirit.

I'm imagining
everywhere I go today
original love —
a mother's love — is with me
and I'm really not alone.

The wood flooring of the Zen temple was
Old and the boards were worn by the feet of
Generations and they creaked underfoot
As we walked mindfully as the footing

Was unsteady and sitting in the hall
Listening to people walking engaged
Me as we practiced quiet watchfulness
Because the stepping was impressive and

As I'm practicing quiet watchfulness
Today I realize how much my mind
Resembles the flooring of the temple
Worn with experience into patterns

As I'm sitting in the hall of my mind
Listening I enjoy the morning sun.

Thought is only thought
and often repetitive —
I want to sit in
a sacred place absorbing
magical emanations.

I thought Zen was in the lotus posture
While sitting all day — for day after day —
At the temple like a breathing statue
With legs crossed and feet on thighs and back straight

I told myself that relaxing would be
A failure and I endured needlessly
Because I hadn't discovered my Zen
Compass — there is no need to be extra

Ordinary that the only reason
For the posture is to position the
Mind to be alert and open like a bowl
As thinking and emotion come and go

Without me interfering so I may
Awake to vagaries of mind flowing.

The world appears
according to the
quality of my
perceptions and
actions.

Everyone is free to think whatever
They want about the end of life but it's
Difficult to see with fresh eyes because
Dogma limits the imagination

But the simple wording of the Dalai Lama —
No beginning no ending — resonates
With me because he's not asserting his
Certainty but embracing mystery

As the faces and voices of people
Who disappeared are lingering in my
Memory Dalai enables me to
Relax by suggesting I only have

To live in this moment this place because
Everything and everyone begins here.

People I don't see
anymore are with me and
we are becoming
a caravan traveling
under a resplendent sky.

I wonder whether I wore silk robes and
Used an ivory comb and selected the
Most beautiful woman and I wonder
Whether I was eloquent and enjoyed

Admiration in society — and
I wonder whether I was bound in chains
And whipped to do a master's work who thought
Me less important than his horse — and I

Wonder whether in playing with words in
Becoming vigorous with exercise
In being compassionate with people
In walking with dignity in modest

Circumstances — I wonder whether I've
Done enough to sanctify this lifetime.

I am creating
momentum as my bodies
dissolve and arise
again and I'd like to think
I'm surfing inspiration.

Thunder before dawn is a drum without
Melody and lightning is a crack in
The dark revealing a fracture in the
Sky at odds with the sounding of the rain

On the roof that lulls and soothes and I'm not
Awake and not asleep but in a trance
Of childlike wonder absorbing the force
Of the night unpredictable and sharp

With clamor and fire as if I'm on the
Edge of battle and doom were in the air
As if violence were imminent and
The covers and the roof aren't protection

As if nothing could shield me from the spears
And the animosity of strangers.

There's not a hint of
my childish fear this morning
as the day is bright
and all that's left of the night
are puddles reflecting sky.

My head is an oven and the heat is
On and kernels of possibility
Are baking and one by one a thought will
Pop in my mind and off I go having

Gained a direction and while talking to
A friend anything I hear will ping a
Response and we will be ponging along
Together and if we have similar

Kernels we'll be popping excitedly
But when I'm in a group I find my mind
Will slip away and I will be searching
For beautiful women nearby because

I have seeds of loneliness baking and
Exploding controlling my direction.

Not one idea
is isolated as each
thought arises from
previous thoughts and I want
to have healthy direction.

In memory there are phantoms as I
Remember how I choose to remember
As I'm not choosing consciously as my
Dreaming personality is making

Choices as my experience is full
Of exquisite detail and today I
Am using an edited version of
Who I think I am — it is easy to

Remember difficulty and failure
But I need a gentle persistence to
Empty negative memories and to
Settle myself on a firm foundation —

While I'm sitting in the lotus posture
I know my heart is as vast as the sky.

The little me is
competing and criticizing
but the big me is
absorbing experience
and transforming.

I remember walking with Joshua
And becoming frustrated with his one
Word responses as he was refusing
To communicate as he was angry

And discouraged as he was putting me
At a distance as never before and
As a dad I wanted to help but I
Couldn't fathom the desperation I

Sensed in him and I didn't know whether
The mood was temporary was teenage
Angst or whether his difficulty was
Dangerous that needed my attention

And as I remembered the brilliant and
Carefree child I didn't know what to do.

I was proud of my
intelligent and cheerful
son but something was
happening and I wondered
am I doing something wrong?

It was a little odd that she would want
To go to Minneapolis to the
Asian food store for a final time the
Day before she had determined to board

A plane bound for her homeland in Japan
After the divorce was certified and
After a twenty-seven marriage
Dissolved because she said there were items

I would need but I discovered that she
Wanted to sit in the back seat and cry
And exercise her anger a final
Time while I drove forty minutes there and

Forty minutes back while I listened to
Music because what else could I have done?

It was her habit
to express frustration with
accusation and
tears and usually I
became quiet and distant.

Because Yoshiko's Dad repeatedly
Took his employers' money and lost it
Gambling on horse races — because her dad
Inherited compulsivity from

I don't know how many generations
Of misery — and because I arrived
In Japan young and ignorant as an
Alcoholic sober for only two

Years — Yoshiko and I were caught in a
Current and we didn't know where we were
Going as we were drawn together as
Her disturbed energy attracted me

As her pattern of behavior was like
A whirlpool circling a black hole.

Yoshiko's anger
escalated exploded
periodically
but I didn't understand
and I believed I caused it.

The rules of a family are established
By force of personality and no
One could get angrier and be angry
Longer than Yoshiko as she set the

Pattern of normalcy and eruption
As it was normal between explosions
To believe everything was OK and
I was proud of being married with kids

And after the anger she was kind and
Busy as long as possible until
Darkness emerged again and she lifted
Her blame shield that allowed her to find fault

Outside herself because it was too hard
To remember painful experience.

Even with sober
friends and meditation I
sometimes didn't know
if I were wrong or right as
we were in a world of hurt.

In a hotel room after her dad took
His employer's money again — after
He spent it at the racetrack — after she
Was married and pregnant — after angry

Managers came looking for payback from
Her and me — Yoshiko arranged to meet
Her Dad to tell him — like her mother and
Sister before her — that she had enough —

This was last time she wanted to see
Him and she wanted no contact and I
Remember how matter-of-fact she was
And I know there was no future contact

And I was a witness after we moved
To America word came he was dead.

We heard he died once
and we heard he died again
in mysterious
circumstances and we
heard he had died in squalor.

Memories are funny as they're buried
Within the mind and I wonder whether
Memories can poison the body as
Yoshiko endured diabetes and

Cancer and I wonder whether she and
Joshua could find solace as I do
In meditation because it seems that
Haphazard forgetting is like trying

To force water uphill and I'd like them
To talk about the phantoms whispering
In their heads I'd like them to understand
Clarity is necessary as I

Have learned to use the lotus position
To let memories arise and vanish.

In meditation
I face phantoms quietly
I let them go as
often as necessary
for acceptance to arise.

After thirty years of sitting in the
Lotus position with my spine straight and
My shoulders relaxed I've practiced breathing
And letting go of thoughts and I like the

Word liberation and I ponder what
It means and pondering is helpful as
I've filtered my memories and my fears
With the magic of peaceful consciousness

But pondering is not enough because
My mind is a bowl and I have to burn
Dispiriting thoughts and have to return
To emptiness as much as possible —

I can be peacefully awake because
I practice letting go of disturbance.

I don't have to rush
into tomorrow in an
effort to escape
yesterday I can take my
time and enjoy my breathing.

I allow my emotions to come and
Go and I understand more about why
Things happened as they did and why I got
Caught in patterns of circumstances but

While I watch the sun touch cottonwood leaves
I'm watching the sun and leaves apart from
Yesterday separate from tomorrow
As there are only leaves tinged with the light

Turning in a breeze and who could want more
And going about my business if I
Stumble into trouble I remember
I can appreciate my breathing as

I have discovered liberation means
Finding simplicity without demands.

In Buddhist sayings
this moment is the one bright
jewel dissolving
time and circumstance and I
have perfect freedom of choice.

Looking back on my time riding buses
On University Avenue from
St. Paul to Minneapolis and back
I remember feeling separate from

Everyone so I speculated on
What people did in the passing buildings
And I took glimpses of faces postures
And different ethnicities and I made

Up stories because I was so young and
Inexperienced and I had no sense
Of direction and I wanted to pierce
Surface appearances and I wanted

To explore the possibilities
But I wasn't ready to open doors.

I took pleasure in
reading philosophy on
austere winter nights
in the warmth of the bus and
no one interrupted me.

Youthful Ambition

I remember taking a bus downtown
With a pen a notebook and a sense of
Mission and I bought a cup of coffee
And I ascended the steps to the Saint

Paul Public Library and I saw the
Stone magnificence and I imagined
The Athenian Acropolis and
I dreamed that my destination was the

Parthenon and I sat in a quiet
Corner under a high ceiling amid
Marble columns with the poet John Keats
On my mind and I marshaled my focus

Because I was determined not to leave
Before I'd written a worthy sonnet.

I fidgeted
I drank coffee
I looked around
at the marble columns but
inspiration escaped me.

Facing a window and television
With the same sportscasters bloviating
At the same time everyday (whom I can't
Hear) there is the elliptical machine

At the gym that I fear and loath because
It draws me and makes me feel cowardly
If I don't get on — and I run like a
Lusty devil for thirty minutes and

I use headphones and music on my cell
Phone for motivation and distraction
And I follow a red dot circling
A racetrack and I watch a timer and

I run through the minutes and rush to a
Crescendo pushing on to exhaustion.

Whether lean or plump
gracefully or awkwardly
many of us are
making circular motions
while not traveling an inch.

St. Croix Crossing Bridge

The designs were contested for fifty
Years because the St. Croix River is a
National treasure that must be preserved —
And the beauty of the limestone bluffs and

The sinuous lines of the serpentine
Valley were taken into account — and
I watched for three years as vast portions of
The earth were repositioned and I heard the

The hammering of the earth making holes
From which the piers were raised and I saw the
Sections of the bridge hanging in air and
Day after day construction continued

And now the valley is refashioned with
The magic of wire rebar and concrete.

The old-fashioned lift
bridge in Stillwater
will be connected
to the Crossing Bridge
with a hiker's trail.

Utopia

Once the idea was accepted that
All means necessary should be taken
For the protection of the earth with the
Support of technological magic

Designers could offer proposals based
On equality and harmony so
Many thousands could live in a single
Sky Tower and the magnificence of

A building in which everyone would be
Given everything necessary and
The elegance of the suggestion that
People would rise above their squabbles and

Hardships to live peacefully in the clouds
Who could resist the enthusiasm?

Designers would need
to discourage obvious
comparisons with
beehives and ant colonies —
who would choose to be a drone?

The idea supporting Sky Towers
Is love of nature and the knowledge that
People tend to despoil the earth so in
Devotion to Gaia people would be

Willing to minimize their destruction
And gather together and the walls of
Their rooms could be pixilated with views
Of a forest a prairie a mountain

And the sensations of outdoors could be
Recreated with the seasons with sun
And stars and frogs in spring and crickets in
The summer nights and there would be no need

For people to roam about the landscape
And everyone could be safe and happy.

And the designers
could monitor the movement
of many thousands
and we could all celebrate
a sky of changing colors.

I've been following descriptions in the
News of architectural miracles
Of towers of steel and glass extending
A mile in height amounting to cities

Containing homes businesses indoor parks
And entertainment centers and what a
Dream for designers of an expertly
Controlled community — but I'd prefer

To live on the ground listening to the
Peeper frogs again in the spring and a
Fountain and a collection of trees on
The eighty-first floor wouldn't be enough

And if there were birds sequestered within
Steel and glass they would be a mockery.

A mile high tower
would make a lovely target
for a terrorist —
with ingenuity he
could detonate a city.

If people chose to live in Sky Towers
The designers would have discretion to
Apportion living space by applying
Flexible standards according to the

Population's preferences and perhaps
An equal distribution of room would
Prevail regardless of merit but some
Would have sunlight and scenery and some

Would live in boxes — some would be high and
Some low and as the disparity of
Property could be narrowed quality
Of life issues would remain because in

Comparison some people always do
Finagle better than most of us can.

How many things do
people really need and if
constrained within a
limited space wouldn't we
be happy with less clutter?

Even though people could be cloistered in
Sky Towers some would refuse to be —
Minerals would continue to be mined
And oil would be drilled and piped and with

The best technology the earth would be
Farmed and the animals slaughtered for our
Consumption — so it's dubious that the
Designers would establish a perfect

Separation of people and nature
But once the bulk of humanity sees
The wisdom of cooperation it's
Possible that we could achieve the dream

Of sustainable communities and
Limit contamination of the Earth.

Because it won't do
to have everyone doing
just as they please — we
need to assure our children
will have oxygen to breathe.

Stripping everything away at bottom
I'm a pink creature with appendages
And when I slide within the curtain and
Step into the shower entering the

Cascading warmth I reacquaint myself
With the bare facts without embarrassment
As if I were apart from scrutiny
As if I were Adam in Paradise

And while soaping and shampooing I watch the
Acrobatics of my thinking as I
Indulge complaints exult successes or
Wallow in guilt and nowhere else am I

As childlike as I am in the shower
Because I become me without armor.

Imagine stretching
yawning and removing
a bathrobe and
absentmindedly
entering Niagara Falls.

Grapes become
the voluptuous girl
luster becoming lust.

— *Tekkan*

www.ingramcontent.com/pod-product-compliance
Lightning Source LLC
Chambersburg PA
CBHW052103070526
44584CB00017B/2312